## FOREWORD

This book is written for two main audiences. The first is the new author. For example, this might be a writer working on, or planning, their debut novel. I hope this book will help writers at this early stage to begin as they mean to go on, with an efficient and long-term way of producing our stock in trade: words. The technique outlined in this book revolutionised my productivity, and I only wish I'd discovered it before I'd struggled through my first couple of books.

The book is also written for authors (self and traditionally published) who share the frustration I felt at writing in fits and starts, squeezing out words between other commitments or, more accurately, *after* other commitments. Weeks of progress followed by months of sporadic inactivity and suddenly a novel that could have been finished in six months has taken eighteen. I've been there, so I know how it feels. This technique will help with that.

Don't make the mistake of thinking that the ten-minute technique is some sort of gimmick. It's actually the foundation of an extremely powerful approach with the potential to revolutionise your productivity. It is based upon the principle that small amounts of effort repeated with absolute regularity can be far more effective than irregular and sporadic mammoth sessions. Think of the blacksmith. Despite what the movies might have you believe, most work with iron is achieved with regular taps of the hammer, shaping the semi-molten metal millimetre by millimetre, second by second until it is transformed into something beautiful and complete.

Read the book with an open mind and give the technique a try by participating in a 28-day-challenge. The least you'll get out of it is a better understanding of yourself and more words on the page than you'd have achieved otherwise.

Good luck!

Kev Partner

www.kevpartner.co.uk

PS: You'll find helpful resources at www.tenminuteauthor.com

# INTRODUCTION

January 19th, 2017 was the day that changed my writing life. On that day, I made the commitment to write for at least ten minutes **every single day**. And, as of this writing, I haven't broken the chain once.

Because of that promise, and the fact that I honoured it, I have written 1.25 million words and published 21 novels, two non-fiction books and many short stories.

I've gone from being an author earning less than £100 ($140) per month to a four-figure monthly income.

I've achieved my dream of earning my living from writing.

But here's the surprising truth: **it hasn't been difficult.** The writing itself is still tough, to be sure. Even after well over a million words, it's hard work because I'm always looking to become a better writer.

But the *habit* of writing is as ingrained in my daily life as walking the dog or making a cuppa.

That is the key.

And it all began on a rainy afternoon in January as I sat in my car waiting for my wife to come out of a hospital appointment.

## Life BTMH (Before Ten-minute habit)

Have you ever started writing a book only to give up part way through?

I have.

Have you ever felt that you'll *never finish* your work in progress? That you're inching your way along, writing words but getting no closer to completion?

I've felt that.

And if you did slog your way through that first draft, have you ever given up editing it because it feels as though the book has no life or merit?

Yep, done that too.

I've been a professional writer since the mid-1990s when I began contributing to PC Pro magazine, the best-selling publication for computer professionals. For the next twenty years I contributed articles that ended up being a monthly 3,000-word column that paid very nicely.

So, I know a thing or two about writing consistently and to a deadline.

And yet, when I decided to try my hand at fiction

for the first time since my teens, I found it tougher than I could possibly have imagined.

I found out about NaNoWriMo[1] in the last couple of days of October 2014 and decided I'd give it a go. The challenge is to write 50,000 words in a month. Now, I have many faults (just ask my wife), but in this case my obstinacy paid off because, despite what seemed like an impossible 1,667 word daily target, I ground it out and wrote that darned book with no outline and very few ideas.

The best I can say about that first draft (which took a further month to finish) was that it didn't entirely suck. The story had some great moments and it did, at least, confirm to me that I could probably write a good novel with practice and training.

But I couldn't get through the second edit. I got bored and concluded that so would my readers.

In 2015, I completed my second NaNoWriMo. This time it was a comic fantasy in honour of Terry Pratchett who'd died that year.

It was much better, but it took another several months to finish the first draft, so I didn't publish this, my first completed novel, until October 2016.

That's almost a year from beginning the first draft. Now, it's fine to take a year *if you're using that time* or if it's intentional. But neither were true for me. I worked on the book in fits and starts when I could find the motivation. I thought lack of time was the problem. **It wasn't.**

In July 2016, while editing book 1, I took a Camp NaNoWriMo[2] and wrote most of the first draft of book 2 in the series. And *that* took months to complete after NaNo was over.

So, I found myself, at the turn of 2017, having taken a little over two years to publish one novel and half write a second.

I knew that I needed to write more consistently, but I was busy with other work that always seemed more urgent.

I tried setting a target of 500 words a day. That lasted two days before I fell off the wagon.

And then I listened to a podcast that featured someone called Stephen Guise talking about the concept of "mini habits". I was intrigued enough to buy the ebook. I devoured it in one sitting—in the car outside the hospital—and decided it was at least worth an experiment.

My wife, who was by this time sick of hearing me moan about my lack of productivity, breathed a sigh of relief as I gushed on about this revelation. And then, with infinite patience, asked whether I was at all interested in how her appointment had gone...

It's no exaggeration to say that beginning this habit marked a turning point in my life as a writer. It hasn't always been plain sailing. Habits can be rocked by things going on in the external world and within my own mind, but as my ten-minute daily writing became more and more solidly embedded, it became harder to shift. It certainly helped that nothing too challenging rocked my world in the first couple of months, but once I'd completed the first 30-day streak, it would have taken a lot to break it.

I'm not saying I'll never take a day off but, so far, I haven't seen the need to. Sure, sometimes the twin demons of procrastination and laziness whisper in my ear, encouraging me to stick the telly on or pick up my guitalele, but I don't listen to them anymore.

It's only ten minutes, after all.

# ABOUT THIS BOOK

THE PRINCIPLE IS BREATHTAKINGLY SIMPLE: *commit to writing for at least ten minutes **every single day** — and then **see that promise through***.

You might now be tempted to throw down the book and start your first ten-minute block and, in that case, I say go for it. But then come back and read the rest. It's pretty short, occasionally entertaining and, as you'll find, there's more to it than meets the eye.

I started my streak back in 2017 based entirely on reading *Mini Habits*[1] by Stephen Guise. Later on, having already written the best part of a million words through my ten-minute habit, I encountered *Atomic Habits*[2] by James Clear which confirmed much of what I was doing, but also helped me add a few wrinkles of my own that I've now incorporated into my routine.

So, in *Ten Minute Author*, I'll spill the beans on my

technique, supported by experience and the research and writings of Guise, Clear and Charles Duhigg.

But this is a practical guide—I'll only cover enough of the theory to help you understand why and how this technique works.

I completely accept that the ten-minute habit won't suit everyone. It's a little like the plotter or pantser debate (see later). Writing is an intensely personal exercise and you need to find what works for *you*. In my view, the best way to do this is to try as many techniques as you can. But you must give each a genuine try if you're to discover your ideal routine.

For the ten-minute habit, I want you to commit to following the technique for just **28 days**. That gives you long enough to try it on for size. Even if you decide it's not for you, you'll end those 28 days with more words than you started, *and* you'll have proven that you can write consistently. You should find those four weeks enjoyable and fulfilling, and I guarantee you'll learn something about yourself both as a writer and as a human being. I suspect you'll like what you discover.

This book also contains many of the craft and productivity lessons I've learned as an author. They're not here because I think I'm some sort of self-publishing guru, but because I know that many readers of this book will be at the beginning of their careers, and I want to pass on some of what I've learned to make their path a little smoother than mine. As with all things indie publishing, take from it what you wish.

## THE WRITER

HABITS FORM OUR IDENTITY, NOT THE OTHER WAY around. A smoker doesn't smoke because they're a smoker; they're a smoker because they smoke.

In other words, *do it to be it.*

This simple truth, which is covered at length in *Atomic Habits*, is nevertheless profound.

A pianist is someone who plays the piano.
A painter is someone who paints.
A writer is someone who writes.
An author is someone who *finishes.*
A published author is someone who shares what they've finished with others.

Now, okay, those last two are my own definitions, but my point is this:

**To be a writer you must write**.

"Congratulations Captain Obvious," I hear you cry, but this is **critical**. Because the corollary to that statement is this one:

If you write, **you are a writer.**

That is the *only* qualification. There are no exams to take and no organisations to join. You don't have to have published a single word.

You simply have to write.

And every word you write reinforces your identity as a writer until you finally become comfortable answering the "what do you do?" question with that response, "I am a writer."

You will continue to be all the other things you are. A parent, a friend, a teacher, office worker or (heaven have mercy on your soul) a tax inspector. But by writing you also become a writer.

I've noticed, after years in the author community, many of my fellow writers struggle with issues of identity. If that doesn't apply to you, then that's wonderful. Feel free to skip over this chapter. As I said in the introduction, I'd been paid to write for over twenty years when I began writing fiction, so I ought to have had confidence in my ability to write, but even I suffered from imposter syndrome and all the doubts that come with that. I can only imagine how crippling it must be for those new to writing (or, at least, new to writing words they want the public to read). The answer for me was to write. Every word strengthened my identity as a writer.

But there's more to it than that.

You see, it's not just about writing. It's about *practising consistently*.

Anyone who plays the piano could call themselves a pianist, but I doubt they would *unless* they felt confident that they could perform a composition in front of others to a *professional* level.

It's the same with writing. If you write, you're a writer. That is your identity. But you're only likely to broadcast that once your writing reaches a professional level. Exactly how you'd define that varies, but, in my view, it amounts to whether a stranger would pay for your words. So, your self-published book becomes professional when someone pays for it. And doesn't immediately ask for a refund.

Well, okay, that's a little simplistic. It's not entirely beyond the bounds of possibility that you might sell a single copy of a book even if it's awful: I don't want to get into the weeds on this. But a professional wouldn't publish a book that wasn't good enough; they'd hire an editor to make sure that didn't happen.

How does the piano player become a pianist? By playing the piano. A LOT.

Malcolm Gladwell, in his book *Outliers*[1], described a study that looked at three groups of musicians. All had achieved a high enough level to be admitted to a prestigious academy, and the study looked into what sort of career this led to. He split them into three groups. At the top end were the virtuosos: the lead violinist in an orchestra, for example. Professional musicians made up the second group. These artists were astonishingly good compared to a ham-fisted strummer like me, but not accomplished enough to be first violinist. And the third group became music teachers. And before I get any hate mail: I didn't invent these categories! Go read *Outliers* for yourself if you don't believe me.

What was the essential difference between these three groups? The amount of time they spent practising. Remember, they were all talented enough to get into the institution, but then went on to vastly different careers.

Some have criticised Gladwell's book because it has been interpreted to mean talent doesn't matter; that enough practice would turn a musical doofus like me into a prodigy. My personal belief is that just about anyone is capable of reaching a decent level in most activities with enough effort, but that getting to the very top of any profession requires the magic ingredient: innate talent.

But here's the point: even the most talented musicians won't succeed without a LOT of practice.

The ten-minute author habit provides structure for that practice. You can bet your bottom dollar I'm a better writer today than I was a million words ago. But

I wouldn't have written a million words *unless* writing had become a daily habit. You might be different. You may be able to write twenty thousand words consistently over the weekends and if you *know* that to be the case then more power to you.

But if you're like most of us, you'll find that little and often is the formula for getting those words under your belt. A messy first draft can, with effort and guidance, become a first novel to be proud of. It'll be your worst novel, but only because you will become a better writer with every word you write.

One final point. You may be wondering how on earth you'll manage a million words if you're only writing for ten minutes a day. The answer's simple—you will write for more than that in practice. **The key is to consider any day on which you complete your ten minutes as a success and a continuation of your streak.**

I'm a nerd so I've kept close track of my progress since I started my daily habit. In 2017, I wrote on average 550 words a day and spent something like 30 minutes writing (usually in two or more sessions). By 2019, this had grown to 1,500 words a day on average. But some days I still only write for ten minutes (especially at weekends).

Remember that I failed pathetically when I decided to aim for 500 words a day, but by focusing on the ten-minute habit, I exceeded that former target comfortably without even thinking about it.

But even if you can only find ten minutes, they stack up over time and those sessions build the habit until it's unbreakable.

# THE HARD TRUTH

I SUSPECT SOME READERS WILL PUT THE BOOK down by the end of this short chapter. Some will take offence (where none is meant). But I'm going ahead with it, anyway.

Let's say you've come to this book because you're not writing as many words as you'd like. Clearly, whatever you're doing at the moment isn't working. You read through to the end, by which point you understand how the technique works and why it can be effective.

And then you put the book down.

You don't commit to the technique for 28 days.

Or, you begin but fall off the wagon at some point.[1]

*What does that say about how important being a writer is to you?*

If, having acknowledged that you have a problem getting enough words on the page, you're not prepared to spend ten minutes a day establishing a habit that could very well entirely resolve the issue, then writing just isn't that important. Well, okay, it's possible that reading this book will pique your interest, but you'll decide this technique isn't for you and find an alternative that does work. In that case, excellent.

But if, in a month's time, you're still not writing as much as you need to, then consider whether you might have been better off giving the ten-minute habit the chance to bed in.

**It's only ten minutes a day**. That's the length of time it takes to eat a bowl of cornflakes.

Some of you will start with good intentions and then come to a point when you really don't want to sit down and do your ten minutes. That's the moment for self-reflection. Ask yourself "Am I a writer or not?" Remember: writers write. **Even when they don't feel like it.**

If you come out of this having discovered something about the relative importance of writing to you, then that's not a complete loss.

But if you *do* want to be a better writer using this technique, then the first step is to make the commitment and the second is to see it through.

Are there any reasons for failing to write for 28 consecutive days? Sure. The world will continue to throw obstacles at you with no respect for your new habit. **But that's the point of making it a**

**habit**—the longer you practise it, the more resilient it is. Of course, emergencies do happen, and in that case it's up to you to decide in each case whether you *truly* couldn't write for ten minutes, because every day you triumph over adversity and bank those words when it would have been easy to give up strengthens the habit far more than the days when it *is* easy.

And every time you don't write the words when you know, in your heart, that you could have done, weakens the habit and undermines your identity as a writer.

As James Clear says in *Atomic Habits*:

> *"Your actions reveal how badly you want something. If you keep saying something is a priority but you never act on it, then you don't really want it.*[2]*"*

So, let's get writing.

# I

## HABITS

# 1

## ABOUT WORDS

IT'S EASY TO IMAGINE IN THE EARLY DAYS OF A
writing career, that words are a strictly rationed
commodity, as if they're drawn from a well that will
one day dry up. This is because writing is **hard**,
especially at the beginning.

In fact, words spring from a more or less limitless
resource. When you've struggled your way through
your first novel of, say, 60,000 words, then it might feel
as though every one of those was an exquisite torture.
But, just like a toddler taking their first faltering steps,
writing becomes easier the more you do it.

The second 60,000 will be easier than the first and
so on until you hit the million that many experienced
authors consider the point at which you have truly
found your voice.

So, every word you write is more practise that will
improve you as an author. Aspects of writing you

found an almost insurmountable challenge become simple and you move onto the finer points of tightening up your craft.

A violinist doesn't ask why they need to practice. Anyone who's ever learned a tune on the violin knows it can start painfully, but in the end your fingers move without thinking. The difference between those two states is practice.

As you move forward in your author career, productivity is likely to be one of the main issues you need to tackle. The more high-quality words you can write, the more books you can publish and, potentially at least, the more money you can make.[1] Crucially, however, you'll be a better writer for producing those words.

However quickly you want to write, I suggest starting slowly and working your way up. I now write 2,500 words per day during the working week, but if you'd suggested I was capable of that when I started my first novel, I'd have laughed at you. And if I'd have taken you seriously, I'd have felt overwhelmed and, unable to get close to that level, I would have bailed out, assuming I was just not good enough to be an author.

There are still many authors who write more than I do, but I suspect 2,500 words a day puts me in the top few percent for productivity.

And the ten-minute habit was (and is) the foundation underpinning this.

## 2

## MINI HABITS

IN THE LAST DAYS OF 2012, STEPHEN GUISE found himself contemplating his lack of fitness, as many of us do at the turn of the year.

For the previous decade, he'd tried various exercise regimens and failed with every single one. I can relate to this, and I suspect you can too. But, not one to give up, he committed to exercising for at least thirty minutes every day, beginning at that moment on 28<sup>th</sup> December 2012.

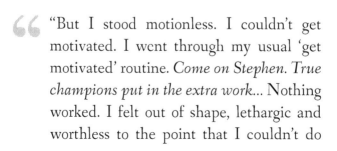 "But I stood motionless. I couldn't get motivated. I went through my usual 'get motivated' routine. *Come on Stephen. True champions put in the extra work...* Nothing worked. I felt out of shape, lethargic and worthless to the point that I couldn't do

anything. A 30-minute workout looked
like Mount Everest. The idea of exercise
was wholly unappealing. I felt so defeated,
and I was."[1]

Guise wasn't just intimidated by the workout itself,
but also by the scale of the effort needed to achieve his
fitness goals. It was as if he was standing at the foot of
the mountain looking up at a seemingly unreachable
ledge and then beyond at the impossibly distant peak
that was his ultimate goal.

Can you relate to that? I certainly can. Let's
imagine you're planning to write your first novel. You
don't know, at this stage, how long it will be, so you
spend five minutes on Google to discover that you're
looking at a minimum of 50,000 words[2]. So, on a rainy
Saturday afternoon, you sequester yourself in the
kitchen, your laptop on the table and the door shut, to
begin at the beginning.

If you're like Stephen Guise, you'll sit there while
the procrastination demon squats in your mind finding
a thousand other things to do before you start. You
finally swat it away and start typing. An hour later,
having been disturbed a dozen times by the kids and
spouse (because it is a universal fact that only writers
respect writing time) you've managed to eke out some
words. You check and find that you've written a little
under five hundred. That's 1 percent of a minimum

length novel. You won't get another opportunity to spend a (disturbed) hour writing until next Saturday, which means it'll take two years to produce even a first draft.

Or you perform that calculation before you sit down and give up without even starting.

So, how did Stephen Guise get past this roadblock on the way to fitness?

In his case, he was inspired by a technique proposed by creative guru Michael Michalko[3] called False Faces. Essentially, this is to consider the solution to a problem by looking at its opposite. This can often give new perspective and insight. Strictly speaking, the opposite of exercising is to do nothing at all, so that would hardly be a solution (mind you, wouldn't it be wonderful if it was?). But the opposite of exercising *a lot* is to exercise *a little*. As an experiment, then, he swapped his failed thirty-minute target for a commitment to do **one push-up a day**.

That seems ridiculous on the face of it. I mean, who gets fit by doing one push-up?

But he decided to do it there and then and, once he was on the floor, he carried on. He ended up exercising for twenty minutes.

As he continued through 2013, he noticed two things:

"First, just a few push-ups a day *does* make a difference in how you feel... Second, I realised that exercise was becoming habitual... I was doing *something* every day."

The push-up challenge was the first mini habit Guise incorporated into his day and he's since added many others. His definition of a mini habit is:

*"A VERY small positive behaviour that you force yourself to do every day."*

It seems ridiculous to suggest that one push-up a day will make you fit or, indeed, that writing for ten minutes a day will turn you into a productive author, but you need to see these commitments as the grit in the oyster—seemingly insignificant on their own, but without which the pearl would never develop.

As it happens, if all you have is ten minutes a day to write, that *can* mount up to a lot of writing over a long period.

Let's say you manage 250 words on average in those ten minutes, and you stick to your habit for a year. That's over 90,000 words in the bank: within spitting distance of two novels.

In one year.

From ten minutes a day.

But you'll almost certainly write for longer. Your ten-minute commitment is there to dispel the procrastination demon, but once it's been banished to whichever circle of hell it inhabits in between writing sessions, you'll almost certainly carry on for another five, ten or fifteen minutes. In 2017, I wrote over

200,000 words from mid-January. And it honestly wasn't hard when taken ten minutes at a time.

To return to the mountain climbing analogy— commit to one step at a time and you'll make it there in the end.

## 3

# THE STREAK

MOST OF US HAVE BECOME FAMILIAR WITH THE old enemy: the procrastination demon. It sits on our shoulder, whispering in our ear, doing all in its power to prevent us from moving towards our goals.

"You don't have time for this."

"Shouldn't you be [insert chore here]?"

"Even if you *do* write anything, it'll be garbage, so why waste your time?"

"Writing a novel is a huge task. You'll probably never finish it, so why not do something easier instead? There's a great series on Netflix."

"How can you be so selfish? You could be with [loved one] right now instead of self-indulgently sitting here pretending you're a *writer*."

Wow, I got a little carried away with that, but my demon and I are well acquainted. These days, it focuses on other things than writing because it knows *that* battle is lost.

Do you recognise some of those sentiments? Of course, the demon is part of your own psyche, not some refugee from the Discworld, but that makes it all the harder to deal with.

In my view, procrastination is often founded on negative emotions and guilt is the weapon of choice when it comes to putting you off writing. There's no point denying that writing is a selfish pursuit, as is any activity that doesn't have an immediate and obvious benefit to others. Procrastination rarely prevents us from going to work because otherwise we wouldn't get paid, but it's a whole different ballgame when you want to *indulge* yourself in a creative pursuit.

"I mean, who do you think you are? Hugh Howey? Your book will probably suck, anyway."

And there it goes again. It's all too easy, isn't it?

The other emotional response is linked to this last round of ammunition. After all, if you don't finish your book then you can't be a complete failure, can you? You've failed to finish it, but you don't risk discovering that you can't write for toffee. Imposter syndrome could be an even bigger issue than guilt. There's no hiding the fact that putting your work out there is nerve-wracking.

But it's also one of the most rewarding and wonderful things you can do for yourself. Because, even in the worst-case scenario that the book gets predominantly bad reviews (which is unlikely if you work with an editor and a group of friendly first readers) that in no way undermines your main achievement: **you wrote a book**. Most of the naysayers gave in to their demon, but you bested it.

So, how do we deal with procrastination? I want to focus on two tools this technique offers that'll shrink your demon to manageable proportions.

The first is the micro-commitment you're making. So, when you begin to tell yourself that you don't have time, your answer should be:

### "It's only ten minutes!"

Writers—including me—can be rather sensitive souls and many of us lack self-confidence, especially at the start of our careers. But it comes to a pretty pass if we think so little of ourselves that we cannot focus on spending **0.7% of a day** feeding our creative souls.

*It's only ten minutes.*

You can do your chores afterwards. You can spend time with the kids in ten minutes time. Just get the writing done and enjoy a minor victory that contributes towards winning the war.

By committing to the ten-minute habit, then, you arm yourself with the first weapon.

The second weapon is the power of the streak. It's been this that has seen me through those moments when I really might have fallen off the wagon.

In 2017, my wife, son and I had been to see Yorkshire folk singer Kate Rusby in concert. It was a wonderful but long evening, and we climbed into bed at around 11.40 pm, looking forward to falling asleep quickly.

In fact, my wife was snoring when I realised: **I hadn't written my words that day**. I have no idea why, given that I used all the techniques I describe later for making sure it happened. I guess I was mesmerised by the prospect of Kate.

As I lay there, it would have been **so** easy to shrug and go to sleep. But, by that time, I'd been writing every day for months.

I visualise the streak as an unbroken chain and, even though I was knackered and wanted nothing more than to go to sleep, I hauled myself out of bed, sneaked downstairs, opened up my Chromebook, started a ten minute timer and got the words in before midnight.

It was the streak that got me out of bed that night, and it was the streak that finally beat my demon into submission.

I predict it'll be the same for you. Once you get past a week of writing every day, that chain will become stronger and longer and harder to break. I've written every day for more than three years because of the power of the streak.

This is why I recommend committing to writing for **ten minutes per day over 28 consecutive days**. I hope that, by the time you finish the four weeks, you'll simply carry that streak on, strengthening it with every passing day.

But, for now, simply make the 28 day commitment. Once you reach that milestone, you can then take it a day at a time.

## 4

# CHUNKING, CUE, ROUTINE, REWARD

CHARLES DUHIGG, AWARD WINNING PRODUCTIVITY expert and journalist, divides the performance of a habit into the three phases: *Cue*, *Routine* and *Reward*. To make a habit stick, you have to get all three working together.

The cue is what triggers the performance of the habit.

The routine is the habit itself.

The reward is how the brain learns whether the habit is worth reinforcing. The reward is critical to success.

## 5

## THE BASAL GANGLIA

Deep within your brain, the basal ganglia are a collection of structures that link you to all other vertebrates from fish to birds. They sit between the brain stem (responsible for controlling unconscious bodily functions such as breathing), and the cerebral cortex which is the "thinking" part of our brain. And they're critical to habit formation.

Do you remember learning to ride a bike? It's a process that, to begin with at least, seems to involve every part of the brain. If you watch a child's face as they're learning, you'll see a look of intense concentration and, after a short time, exhaustion. Bit by bit, however, by repetition and practice, they become more and more adept until, soon enough, they are riding the bike with no conscious effort.

So, what's going on? Well, it turns out that while the higher functions of the mind are working at their full capacity, they're doing two things: burning calories and monopolising bandwidth. Imagine if riding a bike or driving a car involved as much daily effort as when you first learned? It would be utterly exhausting. And, from the point of view of our ancestors on the African plains, being totally absorbed in something makes us less likely to spot the lion in the undergrowth.

Our basal ganglia play a key role in turning these conscious activities into habits. This is a process called "chunking", where a series of actions is brought together into a sequence that is carried out without thinking. Once in place, the brain's conscious activity spikes at the time of the *cue* and the *reward*, but dips during the performance of the *routine*.

This is why we can forget whether we've even performed a habit. People who take regular medication, for example, might keep their pills in boxes with the date on, so they know whether they've taken any particular drug that day.

The evolutionary benefit of this chunking is that it reduces the energy used by the brain and allows for attention to be directed elsewhere. If you've ever got to the end of the day and simply can't make another decision, however trivial, then you know how muddled the mind can get when it's been overburdened.

If you've been paying close attention, you might imagine I've just suggested that once the habit of writing every day has formed, the writing itself (the routine) is automatic. No. In this case, the routine isn't the writing, it's the **getting started**. You do **not** need a habit to help you write, but you do need to form **the habit of starting**.

Our aim then, is to form a daily writing habit that becomes automatic, and so we have to use what we know about the way our brains work to do this. A lot of this will feel like we're trying to trick ourselves, but it's more a matter of knowing how we operate. It's easy to think that we're the summit of evolution with unique and perfectly rational minds, but our brains have been formed over hundreds of millions of years and, while our cerebral cortex is bigger than that of even our fellow apes, it's still built upon structures that first evolved in our fish and reptile ancestors. So, we have to think like the monkey brain we are if we're to win the war of good habit forming.

---

## 6

## JULIO

I'D LIKE TO INTRODUCE JULIO. HE WAS A MACAQUE monkey and the subject of some ethically questionable experiments (if you ask me) that took place in the unenlightened 1980s. Professor Wolfram Schultz (I kid you not) of the University of Cambridge was interested in habit formation, and Julio was his star subject.

A thin electrode had been inserted in the monkey's brain so Schultz could monitor the electrical response to certain activities. In one experiment, Julio sat in a chair in front of a computer screen and learned to pull a lever when he saw certain colourful patterns appear. When he did that, he was rewarded with a drop of his favourite drink: blackcurrant juice.

After many repetitions, the habit settled, and Schultz noticed a consistent pattern in Julio's electrical response—the peak in brain activity coincided with when he received his blackcurrant hit. But as time went on, this peak would occur earlier. In other words, Julio's brain was anticipating the reward by producing the same electrical activity as if he was already drinking it.

I'm sure we've all experienced this. If you're a tea freak like me, then when you've been on a caffeine drought for, say, a few hours, you start getting cranky, but if you pay attention, you'll notice that once you begin the habit of making a cup, the pleasure sensation starts *before* you take your first sip. That sigh of relaxation. It might be the pouring of the boiling water or the wafting of the scent. But either way, you are experiencing the reward of the habit of tea making before you actually drink.

In a similar way, if Julio didn't receive the reward, his response would be to get frustrated and angry. He was experiencing a craving.

To go back to the tea example (you could, of course, substitute smoking, drinking or chocolate), there comes a point when I *have* to have a cuppa, or I'll become even more grumpy than usual. Is this caffeine addiction? Well, caffeine isn't addictive in the strict sense[1] (it doesn't threaten your health if you stop taking it abruptly) but the *habit* of drinking caffeinated beverages and the pleasure they bring is so powerful that denying it can cause frustration.

I remember one occasion when I was particularly

affected. I had been coerced into an afternoon's shopping and the promise implicit in that particular husbandly contract is that I'll get a cup of tea and a slice of something bad for me as a reward for behaving myself. In fairness, my wife didn't forget; it was just that every time we found a café, there was such a long queue we would pass on by to find another. I don't generally suffer from depression, but I felt the distinctive black cloud settle on my shoulders that I recognise as heralding the slip into a funk.

By the time I finally got my cup of tea, my wife would have found the local bridge-haunting troll better company.

Why was it so bad? Because the *cue* hadn't been followed by the *routine* that led to the *reward*.

The cue was the shopping trip. When we go on such expeditions, I expect a cup of tea. But every time we tried to go through the routine of obtaining caffeinated relief, we failed, so I was left frustrated and craving a pot of Yorkshire which manifested itself into extremely grumpy (some would say childish) behaviour.

All over a cup of tea.

Poor Julio. The scientist began messing with the monkey's mind by completely withdrawing the reward, but Julio continued pulling the lever, so ingrained was the habit and so powerful the craving.

So, what does this mean for us as writers? We need

to think about how we can build up this craving that will power our daily writing habit.

And that is entirely dependent on the rewards that come from it. The cue and routine parts are, of course, also important, but without understanding and deeply desiring the *rewards* of the habit, it will not last.

## 7

# YOUR REWARD

WHAT SORT OF REWARDS ARE WE TALKING ABOUT when it comes to a daily writing habit? Each writer will respond to different rewards. This is why it's essential you understand *why* you want to be a writer. There might be more than one reason and it'll be different for each of us.

But if your main reason is to make a fortune, then I suggest looking for another pursuit—making money from fiction, in particular, is *tough*. It can come with time and effort, but if profit is your main motivation, writing might not be for you. And in any case, the reward has to be directly related to the routine. You cannot guarantee you'll make money from your writing and, even if you do, it'll be months, maybe years later. That carrot is not likely to keep you motivated when you're stuck and wondering whether you're any good at all.

Many writers I've spoken to tell me they feel compelled to write, and have always invented stories, but in that case the *routine* itself is the reward. This is fine on those days that you enjoy the writing, but as with any pursuit, there will be days when you don't want to pick up a pen, flip open your laptop screen or grab your voice recorder. And it's on those days that, unless you have a clear aim in mind, you may well break your habit.

Being many days into a streak helps, certainly, and that's saved me more than once, but you also need something positive to fix on during the inevitable dip.

I mentioned identity earlier, and I think it's critical to this. I said that writers write, and writing makes you a writer.

I also said that *finishing* is what transforms you into an author.

It's just my definition, but I think it's a useful one. Writers *write*, authors *finish*.

Don't you want to be an author? **Then you have to finish**.

And the best way to complete your book is to establish a daily habit.

So, your reward for writing today is that you end your ten minutes (or however much longer you wrote) more of a writer than you started it.

**The physical manifestation of that reward is the pleasure of typing your new**

**word count into your spreadsheet or notebook.**

Whether you wrote fifty words or two hundred and fifty, you are now closer to being an author (or more of an author if this isn't your first book).

Pat yourself on the back and glance up at the unbroken sequence of entries above the new one.

Many people use affirmations to help motivate them—for example, "I am an author"—and if that works for you then go for it. But keep your eyes on the prize. **Record your word count** as soon as you've finished your ten-minute stint and you're building a body of evidence that you *can* do this. And, when the imposter syndrome demon makes its inevitable appearance, you can wave your spreadsheet under its nose and cast a banishment incantation.

Having typed my daily word count into my spreadsheet well over a thousand times, I can tell you it gives me the same satisfaction it did on day one. That sense of achievement is my reward. I *am* now an author, but before I published for the first time, much of my motivation was founded on the vision of being one that I kept in my head. For example, being able to type my book title into Amazon and find it there for sale.[1] Seeing reviews. Watching the royalties trickle in. Keep that vision alive and well as you're working towards making it a reality. There's nothing to stop you.

# II

---

# PUTTING IT INTO PRACTICE

## 8

## INTRODUCTION

ARE YOU CONVINCED YET? IF NOT, HAVE ANOTHER read through the earlier chapters. From this point on, I'm going to assume you've committed to the challenge:

A minimum of **ten minutes** of writing **every day** without exception **for twenty-eight days**.

When should you begin? It doesn't matter that much, but it makes sense to spend a few days getting organised, and I recommend starting on a Monday so you'll finish your twenty-eight-day challenge on a Sunday, giving you an opportunity to celebrate. But do whatever makes sense. Starting on the first of the month makes it dead easy to track which day you're on, for example. But if it's now the second, don't delay until next month without good reason (that's your procrastination demon whispering in your ear again) - begin next Monday.

Whatever you decide, **don't kick this into the long grass**. Strike while the iron's hot (two idioms in two sentences, how's that for value?) and commit to a starting date.

## 9

## MAKING IT EASY

THE EASIER YOU MAKE IT TO **START** YOUR ROUTINE (the writing itself) the more likely it is you'll maintain your streak and establish a solid habit. Take this morning as an example. As I write this, it's a Saturday in late March just after the UK has closed schools due to the coronavirus. The sun is shining outside, and from where I'm sitting, I can see the allotments[1] . My plan this morning is to get onto my little plot and do some planting. But I haven't done my ten minutes. The resistance genie (the cousin of the procrastination demon) is telling me how nice it looks and how good it would be to get some salad leaves planted and why don't I just leave the writing until later?

Two things saved me from putting it off and possibly forgetting. Firstly, the streak which is well over 1,000 days now. Secondly, the fact that I've made it easy. I use a Chromebook for most of my writing, and it's just a case of flipping the lid and I'm able to write within moments. So, my ten minutes really *is* ten minutes.

It's so easy, I might as well just get on with it and *then* get my wellies on.

And so, I did.

You're reading it now.

So, much of what we're about to cover amounts to making this habit as easy as possible to keep. One aspect, of course, is that **it's only ten minutes**, but there's more to it than that.

## 10

## YOUR WRITING ENVIRONMENT

I RECOMMEND HAVING SOMEWHERE DEDICATED TO write. In a perfect world, this would be a separate room, but it could be nothing more than a tray with your laptop on it. Having a great writing environment helps make the habit stick. Not having one, on the other hand, is no excuse. Do your level best to make the environment, however basic, something you look forward to inhabiting.

Unless you're one of the hair shirt brigade[1] who prefer to write using pen and paper (or quill and parchment) then you'll need a computer of some sort, with an internet connection.

Which computer? **It doesn't matter**. If it has a keyboard and screen, it'll do. Whether it runs Windows, MacOS or ChromeOS, it'll do. After all, writing a manuscript is functionally equivalent to using a beefed-up electric typewriter:[2] it's about the most basic task a computer can be used for.

So, if you're putting off starting your novel until you can buy that fancy (and expensive) Macbook Pro, then just stop and get a grip! Lots of writers use Macbooks, but it's not the Apple computer that makes them a writer, it's **writing**.

I've written the vast majority of my words on a cheap Chromebook. I almost always buy them refurbed and they suit me perfectly as I like to write using Novlr.org[3] or Dabble. Over time, as I've earned income, I've upgraded to posher Chromebooks with full HD screens (my latest is an Asus C434 if you're interested), but I wrote hundreds of thousands of words on super-cheap equipment.

So, don't put off the ten-minute habit because you're saving up for a new computer—use the one you've got. You could press an old iPad into service if you paired it with a cheap Bluetooth keyboard and, at a pinch, you could even use the same approach with just about any smartphone. Both Google Docs and Microsoft Office offer Android and iOS apps. It may not be ideal, but it **can be done**.

In my view, the environment is more important than the equipment. It's going to be tough to carve out ten minutes unless you find somewhere to be alone, even if that means going out of the house to do it. In a perfect world, you'd have your own room, but that's not practical for everyone. In that case, I recommend having a tray with everything on it ready to go. Whatever you do, try to make your environment as inviting as possible, as that removes one more piece of ammunition from the procrastination demon's armoury.

## 11

## IT'S ALL ABOUT TIMING

You must have an easy to use and reliable way to mark out your ten minutes, even if you intend to carry on writing afterwards. When I first started, I felt my shoulders physically lift when I knew I'd passed the ten minute mark. There was a sense of relief and achievement that, more often than not, gave me the momentum to carry on for a bit.

I've used all sorts of methods, but I began with a simple kitchen timer set to ten minutes. Oh, the sweet music of that buzzer! These days, being a geek, I use Alexa to track my time, and an Alexa Wall Clock to display how long I've got to go. Neither of these is necessary, however. A timer, a stopwatch or an alert on your smartphone all do equally well.

It might seem like a trivial step, but I truly believe that setting a timer is critical to cementing the habit, especially in the early days. Flip the lid on your laptop, open your document, take a deep breath and start the timer. Go!

## 12

## HABIT STACKING

IN THE EARLY DAYS, THE GREATEST DANGER IS simply forgetting. Once it becomes a habit, this is much less likely, but in order to get there, you have to build up a streak of consecutive days. And you can't even blame the procrastination demon if you forget.

One approach is to link the habit of writing to some other, already established habit. I recommend getting your ten minutes done as early in the day as possible since that minimises the chances of forgetting and leaves plenty of time to add some more later. It's also marvellous to go into the day having already achieved something.

So, I suggest finding something you do early in the day and attaching your writing habit to it. This is called *Habit Stacking* and you can use it to link multiple behaviours together.

For example, your commitment might look like this:

"I will write for ten minutes immediately after making my first coffee of the day."

Or:

"The first thing I'll do when I sit down at my desk in the morning is write for ten minutes."

Or:

"Immediately after eating my lunchtime sandwich, I will write for ten minutes."

You should then follow that with the second part of the ten minute commitment:

"Immediately after writing for ten minutes, I will record my word count."

In that case, you might have three habits linked together:

Your morning coffee -> Ten minutes of writing -> Recording word count

As time goes by, you may well discover that the act of recording your new word count and seeing how your daily habit is building up will be reward enough, but in the early days, especially, you can help reinforce the habit with a more tangible reward:

Your morning coffee -> Ten minutes of writing -> Recording word count -> Biscuit

Obviously, substitute your treat of choice. It could be another coffee, or a turn around the block with the dog, glowing in the sense of satisfaction.

What if you want to write for more than ten

minutes? Well, if you're continuing immediately, then do that before you record your word count. If, on the other hand, you intend to come back to it later, then record your count now, have your reward and then update your count later if and when you add new words.

The idea, then, is to find a strong existing habit, something you start without thinking, and attach your new habit to it. The chain can be as long as you like provided it begins with something concrete.

In my case, my cue was sitting at my desk. Since I work from home, I go into my little work area every morning (I operate normal working hours) and arrive at my standing desk. Before I do anything, I write.

I'm a liar.

And I'm ashamed to admit it.

I wish I could claim that I always write first, but the truth is that sometimes I feel the lure of Facebook and spend time on there that should have been spent working. So, I'm not a paragon of virtue. I could get better at this, much better. And yet, even for inefficient me, I still write a **lot** of words, far more than ever before, and my streak is intact. That's because the habit is now ingrained. At the beginning I was rigorous about writing first.

So, give it your best shot. Be strict with yourself until your day doesn't feel complete without doing it. Then you can cut yourself a little slack (but only a little!)

## 13

---

## HABIT INFILTRATION

I'VE DISCUSSED THE POWER OF A STRONG EXISTING habit and how you can link your new daily writing habit to it, but there's another very powerful approach you can use to get started. That's to take an existing habit, keep the cue and reward, but insert a new routine. This is particularly powerful if the existing habit is negative or neutral.

Let's say you've developed a habit of flopping down in front of the telly to watch *The Gilmore Girls* as soon as the kids are in bed. Now, there's nothing wrong with doing this (*The Gilmore Girls* is a masterclass of storytelling), but your primary aim right now is to be a successful author, isn't it? In this case, the cue is putting the kids to bed. However, rather than immediately turning the TV on, I suggest inserting your ten minute writing stint and, when that's done, snuggling on the sofa to find out whether Lorelai has finally seen sense and hooked up with Luke. The cue (the kids' bedtime) and the overall reward (the relaxation and pleasure of watching a favourite TV show) is still there. Even the old routine remains, but a new routine (writing for ten minutes and recording your word count) has been inserted, so you also get the reward for that achievement.

Other habits to hijack include your afternoon break for something sweet (write for ten minutes before cramming the cake), your evening drink or your mid-morning coffee. As long as these things happen every day, they're a good target for inserting your writing habit. If they're not daily habits, then hijacking them means you get extra writing done over and above your ten minutes.

## 14

## CUES, CUES EVERYWHERE

Habit stacking may be enough to make sure you sit down and write every day. Remember, the hard part is *starting*. Writing for ten minutes is comparatively straightforward (you're not aiming to write the next great novel in one draft—this is about establishing the habit), once you've started, you'll finish. **It's only ten minutes**!

However, what if you don't already have a strong habit at around the time in the day when you'd like to establish your writing habit?

That's where visual cues come in. With habit stacking, the cue is the completion of the previous habit. Finishing preparing your coffee leads directly on to sitting down and starting to write, for example. But if you don't regularly start your day with some ritual like this, or you intend to write at a different time, then you need a reminder.

For the first eighteen months of my streak, I had a reminder set via Google Assistant that said, "Have you done your writing yet?" It appeared as a notification on my smartphone at lunchtime and would be visible every time I looked at the phone until, having written for ten minutes, I dismissed it. This approach saved my bacon on more than one occasion.

This was before I'd learned about habit stacking, but I think it's a good backup plan in any case.

Other options include putting post-it notes or postcards in prominent positions you visit every day, especially those you'd see before bedtime. These act as an insurance policy in case your habit stacking and reminders have failed. If you have a cooperative partner at home, you could get them to ask you every evening whether you've done your words.

The more layers of insurance you have, the less chance there is of breaking your streak. As time goes by, you'll be able to relax them, as it'll become entirely natural. Your day won't feel complete until you've written your words and you can then rely on, perhaps, just a reminder from your digital personal assistant of choice as a backstop against the occasional day when, for whatever reason, you've forgotten.

## 15

## THE TEN MINUTES

Right, so you've stacked your habits, eaten your cues and are now sitting/standing at your desk/on your couch, fingers poised over your keyboard/around your pen. You get the picture. What matters is *that* you write not *what* you write.

It's all about the habit. Just as the pianist's first attempts will be ear torture for all involved, their success is based not on that but on the fact that they sat at the instrument and put in their practice time. And that they sat down again the next day. And the next day.

Having said that, I can tell you what my rules are for writing time. Actually, there's only one rule: I must spend those ten minutes writing **new** words. So, reading through a third draft looking for typos does **not** count because it's not writing. Adding new scenes to a first draft, on the other hand, **does** count.

Those who like to plot their novels in advance will have to decide whether that counts. I'm inclined to say it doesn't because I would prefer to spend those ten minutes adding words to my work-in-progress rather than an outline, but as I don't generally work that way in any case, I don't have a strong opinion. All I'll say is that seeing the word count of my first draft rising each day is a huge motivation and one of the reasons I've stuck to the task.

So, get yourself prepared then, as soon as you're ready to start writing, start the timer and **write**. Don't allow anything short of a genuine emergency to interrupt you. Obviously, this means no Facebook (etc.), but your phone should be off or silenced and you **mustn't** be disturbed. If you live with others, you'll need to tell them that you're working for ten minutes and anything they want you for needs to wait for that short period. A sign on the door might also be handy.

You'll have worked out, then, that you are to spend ten minutes writing. The time starts with the first word on the page. So, you might have to spend a minute or two preparing before you begin. But you'll find that, because you're writing every day, your story will always be fresh in your mind, so it really shouldn't take any more than a minute or two to prepare. You've had twenty-four hours to work out a way out of that corner you'd painted yourself into the previous day, after all, so get writing!

Type away for ten minutes and, when the buzzer

goes off, feel your spirits lighten as you've taken one more step towards completing your first draft. Can you carry on? While I was establishing the habit, I found that I carried on for at least ten minutes the vast majority of the time. So, my ten-minute habit produces twenty minutes of writing.

On the other hand, if you've promised the kids that you'll do something for them once you've completed your ten minutes then, of course, you must do that.

Either way, once the writing period is done (even if you intend to write a little more later) then you must record your new word count. This is critical as it forms evidence of your progress that will encourage you as time goes by.

You'll also notice that you're more likely to write for another ten minutes later in the day when you realise how effective it is in getting words on the page, and how easy it is to squeeze into the day.

## 16

---

## BEING STOIC

ONE OF THE UNDERPINNING PHILOSOPHIES OF THE ten-minute habit is that it encourages you to focus on what you *can* control rather than what you can't. Setting aside a very short time to write daily is completely within your power. Setting a daily word count is less so—there are bound to be days when, for whatever reason, you can't quite meet your target, and the first day that happens, your streak is broken and the habit weakened. You certainly can't control whether the book you're writing is going to be a best seller— though you *can* follow best practice.

Do you know the story of William Tell? It's a Swiss legend, but the only part of it that most of us remember is the scene where Tell is forced to shoot an apple placed on his son's head.

The stoic approach to this is to focus entirely on those aspects of the operation that Tell can control. Is the crossbow properly set up? Has he practised? Is he holding it correctly? Is he relaxed? Once he has released the bolt, his control ends and whether it hits the apple, or his son, is no longer something he can influence at all. So, rather than focusing on the outcome of what he's doing, he only concerns himself with those aspects he can control entirely. By doing that, he makes success much more likely because, after all, if he didn't practice, had a poorly maintained weapon and was shaking like a leaf, the chance of hitting the apple are much lower. But he can't control whether a gust of wind deflects the bolt.

You *can* control whether you devote a tiny sliver of time to your writing career every day. You *can't* control whether the results of that work become a bestseller. But, like William Tell, by putting in place systems like a writing habit (as well as editing and marketing), you are giving yourself a shot at it.

So, **do not allow doubts about whether what you're writing right now is good enough to deflect you from the habit**. *It doesn't matter*. Just as when practising the piano, you'll play many bum notes. But it is by establishing that habit of regular writing that you will improve so you have a shot at bestseller status. The primary output from your writing habit, however, is a completed book. Celebrate that success, because simply by finishing, you have entered a pretty exclusive club.

## 17

## WHEN BAD THINGS HAPPEN

Sʜ*ᴛ ʜᴀᴘᴘᴇɴs. Iᴛ's ɪɴ ᴛʜᴇ ɴᴀᴛᴜʀᴇ ᴏꜰ ʟɪꜰᴇ. Two days ago, as I write this, my beloved Yorkshire terrier suddenly became terribly ill, and we had to take the heart-breaking decision to do what was right for him. Now, if you've ever lost a dog, you will know that they genuinely become part of the family and part of the routine of everyday life. This was my second such loss, and the grief is totally overpowering—akin to losing a close human family member. Did I want to write? No. Not remotely. It's impossible to write when you're sobbing.

Two and a half years ago, my dad died. My wife, son and I had moved back to my hometown to help care for my parents a few years before, but the flip side of getting even closer to someone I'd always adored, was that it made the pain even harder to bear. And because I'd been more involved in his care than I would have been had I remained living further away, I had more opportunities for guilt.

Anyway, enough of my issues—we've all been through things that turn our lives upside down.

And please don't imagine that I'm painting myself as some kind of writing machine, but neither of these events broke my streak.

In both cases, my writing diminished to the bare minimum of ten minutes, but I still did it. What I noticed was that by being realistic and forcing myself to write when I would be least upset (e.g. before taking the dog to the vet, and then in the late afternoon of the following day when I'd got a bit of a grip) I not only took something positive out of what otherwise felt catastrophic, but I also got a relief from my grief for a few minutes. On the day of dad's funeral, I spent ten minutes on a spaceship in the far reaches of the galaxy. It was a release. He would not have wanted me to break the chain, after all, and I was able to take one tiny positive thing out of the experience.

**But**. That is just how *I* handled it. When things like this happen, only **you** know what the correct path is. You might feel guilty at spending even ten minutes on your own when your world has been turned upside down. I completely understand. **This is not a competition.**

So, my message is to try to write if you believe it will be positive overall for your mental state in difficult times. If you will come out of it feeling good that, despite everything, you kept the chain intact, then go for it. But no one has the right to tell you how to handle such times, least of all a complete stranger like me.

And it's not only grief that can interfere with your habit. You might get so sick that you can't write, or you might be grappling with a chronic condition. You might experience a mental health episode such that you have to focus all your effort on getting well again.

In those situations, then of course you must prioritise. Your mind is your wellspring, and it's inextricably linked to the body it's part of. First and foremost, they must be protected.

But that doesn't mean you should allow a minor cold to break your streak.

The more ingrained the habit is, the better it's able to withstand the slings and arrows.

So, focus on establishing a rock-solid daily writing habit in good times, so it will see you through when things inevitably get rough.

## What if you do have to stop for any reason?

Make the decision and don't beat yourself up. Then, as soon as you possibly can, start a new streak at day 1. Every day you miss, the habit weakens. This is why I absolutely don't recommend taking weekends off.

My routine is to write the vast bulk of my words

during the working week, and at weekends I may well only spend ten minutes a day, but the habit has been preserved.

It's only ten minutes, after all. Even on a busy family Sunday, it ought to be possible to find ten minutes. Tap it out on your smartphone while you're using the bathroom, if necessary, but don't break the chain.

If you've stopped writing for one of the life-event reasons given above, then cut yourself some slack and get back on the bike as soon as you're ready. If, on the other hand, you simply forgot, then start again the next day.

## 18

## THE TWENTY-EIGHT-DAY CHALLENGE

THE BEST WAY TO KICK OFF YOUR NEW WRITING routine is to commit to the twenty-eight-day challenge. It's very simple: **you will write for ten minutes every day for four weeks**. It's the perfect way to try the technique on for size.

Just like the ten-minute challenge itself, committing to only twenty-eight days shouldn't be something you baulk at. It's still **only ten minutes each day**, but I think it's helpful to have a limit on the commitment to begin with.

If you make it to the end (and you should), you'll be able to reflect on your experience—including your record of how many words you've written over those four weeks—and decide whether you're going to adopt the habit going forward.

Just remember, the ten-minute habit isn't really a

pick and mix technique—it only works if you commit to writing for ten minutes **every day**. If you decide, for example, to take weekends off, the habit is being broken every single week and it likely won't last. Your momentum will be lost, so starting on Monday will be a struggle. And, of course, you're losing almost 30% of your writing time.

I recommend starting on a Monday, so your final day is Sunday and you can have a little celebration. I hope and believe you'll find the habit so useful you'll carry it on. After twenty-eight consecutive days, you already have a decent streak built up—do you want to break it?

My challenge to you is to give this technique a fair try over four weeks. If it works, then keep going, and watch as your word count builds, and you finally have a system for getting your words written.

## 19

## STEP BY STEP

Begin by downloading the printable calendar and word count spreadsheets at **www.tenminuteauthor.com**

**Step 1:** Make the commitment to ten minutes of writing every day for twenty-eight days.

**Step 2:** Make sure you have the equipment you're going to need, and that you have set up a good working environment, however basic.

**Step 3:** Decide when you're going to do your writing. Until it is 100% solid, aim to do your ten minutes at the same time each day. Identify which existing habit you're going to link your ten minutes to. For example, attach it to your morning coffee ritual or immediately on starting work for the day. Alternatively, begin your ten minutes immediately after eating your lunchtime meal. It doesn't matter much, though earlier in the day is better.

Write your commitment in this form: "I will write for ten minutes immediately after I have [existing habit]".

Join the Ten Minute Author group on Facebook by going to **fb.com/groups/10minuteauthor** and find a like-minded set of people all working on the ten-minute habit. Every day at noon (UK time) a prompt is posted for you to let the group know when you've completed your words. This extra accountability can make all the difference on a day when you might be wavering.

### Each day:

**Step 4:** Use a kitchen timer or similar device and start it as soon as you begin writing. Allow nothing to disturb or interrupt you during your ten minutes. Focus entirely on writing new words.

**Step 5:** When the buzzer goes off, decide whether you're going to continue. Once you've finished writing (even if you intend to write more later in the day) **record your word count**.

**Step 6:** Enjoy your reward. At the very least, this should be a feeling of accomplishment, but a little treat wouldn't go amiss.

## After the challenge

At the end of the challenge, calculate how many words you wrote over the 28 days (you'll be surprised—it'll certainly be a lot more than if you hadn't taken part) and then settle down and **read them**. They're likely to be a little rough and ready, but please take satisfaction in knowing, as you read, that these words didn't exist 28 days ago. They came about because you **delivered** on a commitment. You delivered on a small, but regular investment in your career as an author. And like all small, regular investments, they pay off over the long term. Far better to have a modest daily writing habit than to rely on irregular binges. One of these is going to work in the long term, the other isn't.

Then, having patted yourself on the back on your achievement, I want you to commit to continuing your streak. The training wheels are off. You've evaluated the habit and if it worked for you, why wouldn't you carry on? Aim for 50 consecutive days (it's only another 22), then 100. The sky's the limit. The only thing between you and your ambitions as an author is this tiny commitment.

Should you write for more than ten minutes? Of course! But any day on which you write for that length of time is a success. It's another entry in the spreadsheet; a continuation of the streak. I mentioned before that I write 2,500 words a day now that I'm earning a full-time income, but my weekends are still ten minute commitments. It took me a long time to work up to this, and I am able to consistently write 2,500 words every morning of the working week because of the foundation provided by the ten minute daily habit.

And if I can do it, *you* can.

One final note: **DO NOT FORGET TO RECORD YOUR WORD COUNT**. You might think it's an unnecessary extra step, but please trust me on this—you are much more likely to build a rock-solid habit if you record your count after every session.

This is because an uninterrupted column of numbers becomes evidence for the value of the daily habit as the word count builds. And it's the *uninterrupted* part that's critical—once you've got a week or two under your belt, you will not want to see a single blank cell in your spreadsheet.

Recording your word count is the mortar in the brick wall of your new habit. Without it, the entire structure can fall apart. So, **record your count**.

Remember to download resources to help with this from **www.tenminuteauthor.com**

# III

WRITING TIPS

# INTRODUCTION

I hope, by now, to have convinced you to at least give the ten-minute habit a fair go by committing to write for at least ten minutes **every day** for four consecutive weeks.

My aim with the rest of this book is to offer some guidance on getting the most out of those ten-minute+ blocks of time you're carving out. If you're an experienced author just looking for a new technique for becoming more productive, then you may decide to read these quickly and take what you want from them based on your experience.

If you're at the beginning of your career as an author, and especially if you're about to start writing your first book, then you should find these topics especially useful.

Please understand, however, that these are only **my** points of view. I am not a million-pound author (yet), but I do earn my living from writing and I've spent the past several years immersing myself in the online author community discovering how successful authors go about things.

And you know what?

**Every single one is different.**

Because writing is an intensely personal activity and, because we're all unique, we must each find our own ideal suite of techniques. There are very few subjects that all (or even most) authors agree on[1], and however stridently one writer might insist that their way is better or more professional, you can guarantee to find another who says the opposite.

The lesson is: *take what you want from this or any other source of advice.* Unless the idea repels you, then I suggest trialling as much as possible because you might be surprised. And only retain what works.

For the purposes of this advice, I'll assume that you're going to self-publish, but most of what I have to say applies equally if you're seeking a traditional deal.

## 20

## WHAT SHOULD I WRITE?

I KNOW IT'S POOR FORM TO BEGIN THE ANSWER TO one question by asking another, and even worse to ask two, but I always was a bad lad.

*Question 1: Is this your first book?* If the answer is 'yes' then chances are that you already have an idea—it's what inspired you to think about being an author. In that case, I suggest going for it. Write your passion project. Use the reservoir of motivation you have for it to see you through the inevitable dips.

My first published novel was a comic fantasy in the tradition of the *Discworld* series. I've always written funny stuff, right back to poems about guinea pigs to amuse my classmates at school. Yes, really. I even read them out loud before the teacher arrived:

*And he ploughed through the snow with a bottle of Crusha,*

*Well, what do you expect on a cliff-top in Russia?*

Indeed.

I was only eleven or twelve, however.

Anyway, so when Terry Pratchett died, I decided I would write a comic fantasy novel because it was my favourite genre and because his death had affected me.

If I were starting a ten-minute habit today, I would still write that same first novel—but I'd do it a lot quicker than my haphazard approach of fitting it in with my other commitments. When I felt like it.

*Question 2: Do you want to make money from your writing?* Then do your research in advance. You'll hugely increase your chances of success if you write in a specific genre (cross-genre mashups can be a tough sell), so think about your current idea and work out how it could fit. Do this by identifying the general genre you're writing, then narrowing it down to a specific subcategory. For example, your main genre might be science-fiction, and you identify that it fits into the Galactic Empire subcategory on Amazon. Furthermore, it includes alien characters, so you can target that sub-sub-category.

More likely you'll find a category close to what you intend to write, but you'd need to make a minor course correction. Perhaps put some pirates in there to target that sub-sub-category.

For writing commercially, then, it's generally a matter of writing what you love, but with an eye on meeting the tropes of a niche genre. Romance readers expect a "happily ever after" (HEA) and most romance titles will follow one of a limited number of patterns. This is true of all genre fiction. To have the best chance of commercial success, you'd need to thoroughly research your niche by reading lots of books, and then write a story that satisfies the requirements you discover.

This isn't the place to go into this in depth but take a look at K-lytics[1] for market information.

Having said all that, as I mentioned earlier, in my view the overriding concern when working on your first book is to write what you want. It *will* be your worst book (because you will improve further with practice), but it will also be **finished** and that is an achievement few people can claim.

## 21

## PLOT OR PANTS? HOW I WRITE

THERE ARE MANY TOPICS THAT MOST AUTHORS agree on, so let's focus on something that divides us: should you plan your book before starting, or should you take your basic idea, let your characters loose and see where it takes you? In other words, should you plot, or should you fly by the seat of your pants (otherwise known as discovery writing)?

The short answer is that you should do whatever works for you. Writing is an intensely personal process and the only way you'll discover the best method for you is by trial and error.

A quick poll of my favourite authors reveals that roughly half of them are or were "pantsers": including Stephen King, Terry Pratchett, Isaac Asimov and Bernard Cornwell. JK Rowling is at the other end of the spectrum since she meticulously planned her novels.

**So, clearly both methods can work**.
Despite this, many authors believe that their method is
the right one, the professional one. Indeed, it may seem
logical to plan the book before you begin and, if that
works for you then absolutely go for it, but my brain
doesn't work that way. Writing is **not** a logical process
for me. I *do* occasionally outline—most often when I'm
working with a collaborator and even then only for the
first book in a series—but 90% of my fiction is pantsed.

I think, in some cases, writers confuse the problems
caused by their lack of experience and knowledge with
the technique of pantsing. They talk about writing
themselves into a corner or creating such a messy first
draft that they had to undertake endless rewrites.
These, in my view, are not necessarily issues with the
technique. Neither of these has ever happened to me: I
write clean first drafts quickly. Why? Practice, for one.
And because I have learned story structure.

The idea that I sit at the blank page with no
thought of what comes next and just spew words is
ridiculous. Let's say I'm writing a six-book series. I will
have been mulling over the general thrust of that series
in my mind for weeks. I'll also have thought about the
characters and setting. For example, if I had come up
with the idea of the remake of Battlestar Galactica as a
series of novels, then I'd have the concept of the Cylons
and humans; the ancient ship and having them
shepherd civilian vessels.

When I sit down to write each book, I'll know

where it begins (after the previous book in most cases). I'll know that if each book is going to be sixty thousand words, then I need to set my characters on their journey within the first ten thousand, have a false victory or false defeat at the half way point, have the dark before dawn moment at around 80-90% and then wrap it up. So, my thoughts are on steering the narrative towards the next waypoint rather than planning out those steps in advance.

Why do it this way? Because it works for me! My absolute favourite aspect of writing is when something serendipitous happens. For example, my protagonist encounters a throwaway character who turns out to be the key to everything. Many of my most (apparently) cunning twists or reversals come from this sort of lightning strike, as well as many of my most memorable characters.

So, should you discovery write rather than outline? **No, not if outlining works for you**. I'm merely saying that I think we owe it to ourselves to try different techniques constantly. As I mentioned, I still occasionally outline, even though I'm very comfortable pantsing.

If you're interested in trying either, my go-to book for story structure is *Save the Cat! Writes the Novel*. It's based around the principle of outlining the book, but you can take it or leave it once you understand the structure.

There are tons of books on plotting, but very few

on pantsing specifically. Stephen King's wonderful *On Writing* covers much of his process, but the best book for discovery writing is by Dean Wesley Smith: *Writing into the Dark*.

As a final note, bear in mind that we're talking about a continuum here. Some plotters limit themselves to a very basic framework for their novel whereas others write down every event before starting. Some pantsers incorporate aspects of very high level outlining.

The point is to continue working on your technique until it fits you like an old pair of slippers. And, **if it works for you, then it is right for you**.

## 22

# HOW LONG SHOULD MY BOOK BE?

THE TRITE (BUT TRUE) ANSWER IS *AS LONG AS IT needs to be*. No longer, no shorter.

*David Copperfield* by Charles Dickens is one of my absolute favourite novels. I listen to the audiobook (read by Martin Jarvis) at least once a year and never tire of it. Except for the last few chapters. Dickens had the unusual problem of publishing in weekly instalments as he wrote which meant that he had no way of changing an earlier chapter after publication. He was not an outliner in the sense that we use the term today, but rather kept notes as he worked on each instalment; notes that dealt both with that chapter and future ones.

I know the verbose nature of Victorian prose isn't to the taste of all twenty-first century readers, but I relish it when it is driving the narrative forward. Unfortunately, with *David Copperfield*, Dickens ran out of story with several instalments to go. This results in an overlong ending that features a resolution to just about every character's arc, however insignificant. It would have been an even better book if it had been that little bit shorter.

It still went on to be one of the great novels of the English language, of course, but here's the harsh truth: neither of us is Dickens.

JK Rowling's later books could have done with a bit of a trim, some would say (I love them, personally, but even I got fed up with the quidditch world cup). But we're not Rowling either.

As you become more experienced, you'll get better at judging your pace, and it makes sense to look at other books in your genre to see what readers expect. In general, for example, readers of epic fantasy are looking for a longer story than those of regency romance. But even within that, there's a ton of variation. David Gemmell rose to success writing relatively short epic fantasy, for example, but by having a guide to length you can ensure you don't stray too far from the yellow brick road.

The quickest way to establish the length of the bestselling books in your genre is to buy a K-Lytics report, but you can also estimate it by going to the Amazon pages of your closest bestselling competition and looking for *Print Length*. Multiply that number by three hundred to get a rough word count.

For example, let's say you want to write an epic

fantasy. You work out that the average length of similar books to yours (those that are selling well, anyway) is 100,000 words. Whether you're outlining or pantsing, you now know that you should aim to hit the midpoint at around the 50,000 word mark and begin moving towards the climax from 80,000.

Does it matter if the midpoint happens at 60,000? Nope.

40,000? Nope.

20,000? Yep. Because 120k or 80k isn't a problem. 40k might be for that genre.

That's not to say that a 35,000 word story won't succeed in epic fantasy, but that it's one possible reason for a reader to pass over your book. Selling books is hard enough even with everything in our favour.

But what if you're aiming for 100,000 words and you find yourself only just reaching the midpoint when you pass the six-figure word count? Assuming you haven't spent too many words describing the secret ways of hobbits[1] and can't, therefore, move 35,000 words into an appendix, then you have a couple of choices. You could carry on and write a book of 200,000 words. You could find a way to make a false victory or defeat occurring at the midpoint into a climax and split the story into two books. Or, you could expand the plot to make a trilogy. Which is right for you will depend on the story itself and your plans. Creating a trilogy will take longer (and assumes the story will support it), but epic fantasy readers like trilogies, so it may well sell better than a single 200k book or a pair at 100k each.

Remember that *The Lord of the Rings* is a single story split into three[2] because of the cost of paper in post-war Britain, and yet Tolkien managed to give each something of an ending.

But, in the end, it's all about the story. As you become more experienced, you'll be able to manipulate the pace better, but in the early days, you should let the story take you where it wants to go, while being aware of story structure.

## 23

## BASIC STORY STRUCTURE

THERE ARE MANY GREAT BOOKS ABOUT STORY structure, and there's some logic in educating yourself about it before starting your ten-minute habit. **However**, that could be a dreadful source of procrastination. You will never learn enough about the craft to be truly ready, and the longer you spend in the weeds, the more likely it is you'll miss the opportunity to do what writers do: write.

So, in this section, I'm going to give you the barest of bare bones. I hope this will help form a foundation for your words without bogging you down. Remember, this is primarily about establishing the habit.

The best book about story as a whole, in my view, is *The Writer's Journey* by Christopher Vogler. This is an expansion of Joseph Campbell's *The Hero's Journey* from the point of view of actually writing stories rather than just analysing them. It's a mighty tome, and I think all authors would gain by reading it (even if they don't agree with everything Vogel says) but doing so is a major project. Perhaps you could set up a ten-minute **reading** habit to get through it in short chunks.

My favourite plotting book is *Save the Cat! Writes the Novel* by Jessica Brody and based on the screenwriting classic *Save the Cat!* by Blake Snyder. I recommend this book whether you're a plotter or a pantser: discovery writers have to know story structure just as well as outliners. This book is much more concise and practical than Vogel's, so it would be first in my "to read" list if I were a new author.

For now, however, I'm going to reduce the structure it proposes to the barest essentials so you can get cracking with your ten-minute writing habit. I'm going to use the example of a 60,000 word novel since that's a very common length and it makes the maths relatively simple.

StC uses the classic three act structure with the second act occupying 60% of the word count (36,000 words). Broadly speaking, Act One (12,000 words) takes place in the protagonist's current reality, Act Three (12,000) is the transition to the new reality and Act Two is what happens to set that up. Sometimes, Act Three is a return to the old reality, but it is generally changed. Frodo returns to The Shire, but it's not the same as it was.

For example, in *Harry Potter and the Philosopher's Stone*[1] the first act is spent with the Dursleys, the second act begins when Harry boards the Hogwarts Express. Act Three starts when Harry, Ron and Hermione decide their only option is to go after the stone themselves. The new world that emerges from it is a world where Voldemort is back.

So, the job of Act One is to turn the protagonist's current world upside down and force him or her reluctantly onto their journey (think of Frodo receiving the news from Gandalf that his ring is the One ring).

The first half of Act Two leads up to the midpoint of the novel where the protagonist is working towards what they think is their goal. They will either succeed (false victory) or fail (false defeat). Frodo believes his task is to deliver the ring safely to Rivendell, only to discover that he's actually only just begun his journey (making it a false victory). This is roughly halfway through *The Fellowship of the Ring*. In the middle of the first Harry Potter book, Harry becomes the youngest quidditch seeker in yonks, and helps his team win their match, seemingly achieving all he wanted. Again, this is a false victory because his true task is to unmask Quirrell and face Voldemort.

The false victory or defeat becomes the catalyst for the protagonist to work out what they *really* need to do, and the second half of the second act describes their attempt to do it.

The third act kicks off the climax and the transition to the new world order. In *The Fellowship of the Ring*, it begins with the company leaving Lothlorien and climaxes with Frodo's confrontation with and escape from Boromir. The new reality is the breaking of the fellowship. In that third act, the protagonist must face his or her greatest fears, appear destined to fail and then pull victory from the jaws of defeat.

So, that's a classic story structure. It's not the only one, but it's the most common and the safest foundation for a first novel.

Do you have to use it? **Absolutely not**. You're the author. But it helps to know the rules before you break them. If you want to write something that has a different structure entirely, then all power to you; just acknowledge that it's riskier than a form that has endured for thousands of years.

If you're starting your ten-minute habit at the beginning of a new story, then, you should focus on what is going to happen in that early part that will force the hero (who must be reluctant) out of his or her comfortable normality and onto the path to adventure.

## 24

## WHICH SOFTWARE SHOULD I USE
## FOR MY FIRST DRAFT?

FOR THE TWENTY-EIGHT-DAY CHALLENGE, IT doesn't really matter. As with so many other aspects of the writing life, which software you end up using in the long run is a matter of personal preference.

When I surveyed authors, I found that around 40% of them use Word, 40% Scrivener and the remaining 20% was split among a wide range of tools. I've used just about all of them, and I use different software for different projects.

My fiction first drafts are written using Novlr.org[1] or Dabble[2] Personally, I much prefer using a browser-based writing environment because it gives me the flexibility to use my desktop, Windows laptop or Chromebook (though 90% of my writing is done on the latter). I've also written using Google Docs, but that becomes slow to load once the document gets large and splitting it so that each chapter is a separate document is an exercise in aggravation.

The first draft of this book was written using Word. If you're a subscriber to Microsoft 365 (formerly Office 365), then you have access to an online version of Word that means you can use the full version when working on a desktop or laptop, then open the same document online and carry on where you left off. It's pretty basic, but it does the job. And the reason I'm using it rather than Novlr or Dabble in this case is simple: the online version of Word supports footnotes and Novlr and Dabble don't[3].

I have used Scrivener for non-fiction in the past because it makes it easy to move sections around, but I find it increasingly frustrating and the lack of an online version is a deal breaker for me.

Novlr offers the most enjoyable writing experience (for me), and that matters when you think about how long you spend looking at that screen when you're working on your first draft.

What about later drafts? Most authors I know switch to Word for editing since almost all editors insist on it for its brilliant revision tracking. From a cost point of view, therefore, since you're likely to need Word for editing, the cheapest option is to invest in just that and do your writing in that as well. But for me, the few dollars a month I spend on my Novlr subscription is worth it given the hundreds of hours I use it for.

I encourage you to experiment with lots of

software. I used Google Docs for my first novels, then Word, and I tried Scrivener, LibreOffice and StoryShop among others until I realised they weren't for me.

For now, however, I suggest choosing whatever you're most familiar with for your twenty-eight-day challenge, whether that's Word, Google Docs or whatever.

## 25

## KEEPING NOTES

You shouldn't interrupt your ten minutes of writing by researching or making extensive notes but, on the other hand, if you think of something you'll need to work on later, it makes sense to indicate it at the time. Let's say you're writing a scene set in a bar. What's the bar's name? You may already know, but if you don't, rather than wasting part of your ten minutes on this, you can instead use a placeholder.

For example:

*She'd told Sam to meet her in [coffee shop] at noon, and her stomach tightened as she strode through the open door and squeezed past the queue. She scanned the dark interior, eyes flitting past Apple logos and ponytails until she saw him. He was smiling. Well, she'd soon fix that.*

By popping the missing name between square brackets, you're able to leave that decision to later. You can do the same thing with all sorts of information including character names, incidental facts and time calculations. In the introduction to this book, the second sentence looked like the following right up to a few days before publication:

*Because of that promise, and the fact that I honoured it, I have written [words] and completed [novels].*

Sometimes, however, you need to make a quick note while you think of it for fear of it evaporating. I use Google Keep [1]for this sort of thing. It's free and very easy to use. I have categories including character info, research and world building. I can switch straight to it by going to keep.google.com and spend no more than thirty seconds making the quick note before going back to my writing.

The main thing to remember is to reduce this to an absolute minimum. Use the square bracket technique wherever you can. The key is to keep it simple.

## 26

## DO YOU NEED AN EDITOR?

THE SHORT ANSWER: YES.

Although, as I've said before, I don't generally like absolutes of any sort, it's hard to see how it would be possible to create a professional manuscript without involving a competent third party.

At this stage, however, your aim is to simply write for ten minutes a day and worry about quality later. I'm including my thoughts on editing here, so you get a big picture view and in the hope that you'll relax and push out your first draft without worrying too much about quality at this stage. Editing is a *process*, not a single task, but it needs words on the page and the ten-minute habit is a way to achieve that.

What if you can't afford to hire an editor? Well, the harsh (but fair) response is to save up. By the time your book is ready, you will have spent hundreds of hours on it and it makes no sense, having invested all that time, to publish it in an imperfect state. Furthermore, readers have the right to expect a professional product and they will punish you with a poor review if you shortcut the process.

Having said that, I'm a bootstrapper and skinflint at heart and I recognise that many authors are working on an extremely tight budget. I certainly was at the beginning. And I'd be an utter hypocrite to insist that you should spend a fortune on an edit when I didn't in the beginning.

So, my advice is: get the best editing you can afford. Even if that's a cheap editor on Fiverr, the involvement of a competent third party will result in a better book than if only you go through it.

Here's my process. I write my first draft and then immediately go back through correcting the many typos, tightening the prose and looking for obvious errors[1]. I give that draft to my editor. Her role is restricted to grammar, punctuation and spotting obvious errors in the story because that's what I need at my current stage. I also send that copy to my team of beta readers. I then go through the recommendations of the editor and beta team and choose which I'm going to implement[2]. My wife gets that amended copy to proofread (the third draft). Finally, once I've had her changes, I then give it one more read through from start to finish and the book is then published.

No book is perfect, and pursuing perfection just becomes a form of procrastination, so it's essential to have realistic expectations, but by hiring professionals, you will reduce remaining errors to the absolute minimum.

## 27

## TYPES OF EDITOR

So, MY VIEW IS THAT EVERY BOOK NEEDS competent third party input, but this can take many forms.

### Developmental

The most expensive form of editing, a developmental editor will focus on the structure of your story, plotting, pacing and character development. Using a dev editor might well be a baptism of fire, but it's also probably the most efficient way to become a better writer as long as you focus on learning from the experience. You may well find that you only need a developmental editor for your first couple of books.

The problem: developmental editing is a labour-intensive and highly specialised task, which makes it bloody expensive. I would view any quote from a developmental editor that was less than four figures with extreme suspicion.

If you don't feel you can afford a $2,000 edit, then I hear you. I have never used a developmental editor for exactly that reason. The good news is that there's a much cheaper alternative—become a master of story. Instead of investing money, invest copious amounts of time reading all the classics of story structure and other aspects of the craft. If you can master this, then you don't necessarily need an expensive developmental editor as much. If you can afford a dev edit—especially for your first novel—then it's worth it, but if it was an absolute requirement, I would never have even written my first book because I simply didn't have the means to invest that much money.

In short—your book will be better for the involvement of a good developmental editor, but that doesn't mean it's impossible to write a great book by other means. Whether you use a dev editor or not, you need to become proficient in the craft, but having one will speed that process. My trilogy—the first books I wrote—would certainly have been better for the involvement of such an editor, except that they would never have been written at all because I couldn't find the $5,000 cost of editing three books.

Oh, and if you're an editor yourself, then feel free to disagree. This is just my personal perspective.

. . .

## Line editing

Typically, line editing (like developmental editing) focuses on the story, but it does so at a more detailed level. It won't, generally, advise on structure; it's more about how you communicate the story to the reader. A line editor will usually give advice on aspects of the story that don't work, but most of their input will be around the use of language. They'll point out inconsistencies, issues of pacing, bland wording and suchlike. As with a dev editor, if you engage positively with your editor, you will become a better writer and, over time, you should be able to save money since your editor will have to do less work.

## Copy editing

A copy editor focuses on technical issues. You can expect your copy editor to pick up poor grammar, spelling and punctuation. He or she will help ensure you're consistent in your use of style conventions. Most copy editors use the Chicago Manual of Style[1] and in the early part of your career, it's probably best to take their advice because, frankly, you've got enough plates to spin. As you gain more experience, however, you'll develop your own style and that may involve deviations from CMoS, or you might choose to use spelling variants. As a curmudgeonly old sod who has always spelled *alright* that way, my editor knows not to 'correct' it.

You can expect to receive back a manuscript with many, many tiny edits. Mine tend to be mainly related to commas since they're a particular blind spot for me.[2]

As with dev editing and line editing, you can learn a lot from the changes your editor suggests which will make you a better writer requiring lighter/cheaper edits in the future.

## Proofreading

This isn't really editing at all. In traditional publishing, proofreading takes place once the manuscript has been typeset. The proofreader checks those pages against the original manuscript to make sure no errors have crept in during the formatting process.

In independent publishing, especially of ebooks, most of us consider proofreading to be simply a final check before publishing. In that sense, it's similar to copy editing, since we're generally looking for those final few typos and grammatical errors.

Proofreading is the least risky part of the process to outsource to a non-professional since they're simply spotting errors. My wife performs this function for me.

## Does every book need all of these edits?

No. This is partly because they overlap. If you've hired a developmental editor, you should not need a line edit, though you will still need a copy edit and proofread.

Of course, this all means spending a lot of money. It's not for me to advise you on this except to repeat my feeling that authors should have the best editing they can afford.

If you're on a strictly limited budget, the bare minimum is a copy edit and proofread, in my view. If you can stretch to a line edit also, then that will be well worth it.

## How to find an editor

If at all possible, find an editor who has been recommended by someone you know and trust and who works in the same genre as you[3]. You can also ask in any online communities you're a member of[4]. Failing all that, take a look at Reedsy.com for vetted editors—bear in mind, however, that you'll be paying top dollar for them.

Whoever you choose, I suggest getting a sample edit of a chapter or two. Many editors will provide this free of charge but, in that case, it's only fair that you limit your request to those you're likely to go with rather than getting lots of sample edits.

As for how much to pay, that's going to depend very much on the experience and quality of the editor, the length of your manuscript and your skill as an author. To a degree, you get what you pay for, but you can get good value from someone new to the game, as long as they're competent (recommendations and sample edit will help there).

The professional organisations that represent editors recommend that they charge per hour rather than per word, and I support them in this. If I provide a clean manuscript, I expect to pay less than someone submitting word vomit. However, on receiving sample chapters they ought to be able to provide an estimate.

As a very, very rough guideline, for a 60,000 word manuscript in decent condition, you might typically get quotes of around $1,750 for a developmental edit, $850 for a line edit, $500 for a copy edit and $250 for a proofread. These are just so you get a broad idea since the figures can vary hugely.

## TIPS FROM OTHER AUTHORS

I'VE ASKED A LOT OF EXPERIENCED AUTHORS FOR their top tips for those in the early part of their career. Here's a summary of what they had to say:

1: **Write**. A blank page does nothing to further your career as an author. There is such a thing as too much preparation (it's called procrastination). If you wait until you're certain you're ready, you might never start. With every word, you become a better writer. The whole point of the ten-minute habit is to get you writing.

2: **Finish what you start.** However crappy you think your work in progress is, you **must** finish it, because by doing that you prove that you *can* finish. And you'll also be a better writer for the practice.

3: **Learn the craft.** While you're working on your first draft, you should be reading craft books or taking courses. Don't use this an an excuse to put off starting: your learning will be more effective if you are writing alongside your learning.

4: **Read**. As Stephen King said: "If you don't have time to read, you don't have the time (or the tools) to write." By reading the best fiction in your genre (assuming you're writing fiction) you not only learn from the masters in your field, but you're also conducting market research. What motifs come up often, for example? Maybe your idea is clichéd? Better to find out now than after publication.

5: **Have confidence and humility**. Authors tend to oscillate between two states: thinking that what they're writing is rubbish and believing it's the best thing since a hundred chimps got behind typewriters to come up with Macbeth. Have the confidence to know that with effort you are capable of producing commercial quality fiction. Have the humility to accept that you will never know everything.

6: **Find a support community.** One way or another, you're going to need help at some point. You'll need an editor and proofreader, and you may choose to use beta readers, but there's a lot to be said for joining a community of authors all pursuing the same thing. I'm a member of the SPF Community group on Facebook, so you'll find me there, as well as at the Ten Minute Author group. If you prefer face-to-face meetings, then look for a local writer's group. But whatever avenue of support you opt for, take care that it remains a positive and healthy part of your writing life. Don't be afraid to move on if things turn sour; there are plenty of alternatives. It can be a lonely life, this writing lark, and nobody understands an author like other authors.

## FINAL THOUGHTS

I HOPE THAT, HAVING REACHED THE END OF THIS little book, you're now raring to go. I hope you'll bite the bullet and immediately establish your ten-minute writing habit, or at least make a firm commitment to a start date in the next week or two. By all means prepare, but don't procrastinate. For it is procrastination, not perfection, that's the true enemy of done.

I've published this book because I've experienced the power of writing our stories down—whether they're fiction or non-fiction—and I want to help other authors achieve their aim of finishing their manuscripts. It's one of the most fulfilling things you can ever do.

I hope you'll finish this book feeling confident and inspired to share the gift of your creativity with the world.

# NEXT STEPS

You've made it (almost) to the end of this short book, but I've got a couple of things for (as my American friends term it) extra credit. In the UK, we'd probably call it brownie points, so take your pick.

I hope these will help you get more out of your new habit.

- Go to signup.tenminuteauthor.com/reader and join my reader's group. As I add to this book, I'll send you a free copy of the new sections or updates, plus new resources as I add them. Even if you've already signed up before buying the book, please sign up again so I know you actually bought it and you therefore qualify for extra goodies.
- Pop over to

fb.com/groups/10minuteauthor and join our ultra-helpful community of people using the ten minute habit to boost their productivity.

- If you can't find an answer there, feel free to email me at author@kevpartner.co.uk. I'll be happy to hear from you.

- **Pretty please: add a review if you possibly can**. This helps others decide if this book is worth them reading. You can find links to the book here: www.kevpartner.co.uk/project/ten-minute-author

- Pop over to www.tenminuteauthor.com to check for new resources, updates and downloadables (sign up to the reader's group to be notified of these by email).

## ABOUT ME

I IDENTIFY MOST AS A FATHER, GRANDFATHER, SON, brother and uncle. Born in London in the mid 1960s, I was brought up in the south of England in a wonderful, nurturing environment completely free of the usual fiction clichés. I began writing in my teens, and after a soul crushing time as a junior bank clerk, embarked on my career in communication in the early 1990s. I spent the next eighteen years developing interactive training using laserdisk, floppy disk, CD-ROM and internet. During that time, I also became a freelance tech journalist writing hundreds of thousands of words for computer magazines.

My first books were all traditionally published non-fiction on business topics and my second love (after writing) computer programming.

In 2014, I wrote my first draft. In 2016, I published my first novel. By late 2017, my first trilogy was complete, and I embarked on the six book Robot Empire series that was my first taste of success.

Since 2018, I've worked with Mike Kraus, bestselling author of post apocalyptic fiction, as well as publishing a successful book on how to start up a candle business (my wife and I ran such a company for many years).

In 2017, I also founded IndieAuthorPlatform.com, a company that creates gorgeous websites for authors at an affordable price.

Find me at **kevpartner.co.uk** or **fb.com/kevpartnerAuthor**.

And, of course at **tenminuteauthor.com**.

# NOTES

## Introduction

1. National Novel Writing Month. Every November, hundreds of thousands of authors around the world accept the challenge of writing the first draft of a 50,000 word novel in those thirty days. It's a fantastic experience and I highly recommend it. https://www.nanowrimo.org
2. An informal event where you set your own word count target – I opted for 50,000 words again.

## About this book

1. https://www.kevpartner.co.uk/mini-habits-smaller-habits-bigger-results/
2. https://www.kevpartner.co.uk/atomic-habits-by-james-clear/

## The Writer

1. https://www.kevpartner.co.uk/outliers-by-malcolm-gladwell/

## The Hard Truth

1. Without an exceptionally good reason
2. *Atomic Habits*, Appendix 1, page iv.

## 1. About Words

1. Yes, some people make lots of money from just a few books, but there's a strong correlation between books published and earnings overall. Bestselling authors tend to have a big back catalogue, though having a big back catalogue doesn't guarantee bestselling status.

## 2. Mini Habits

1. Mini Habits by Stephen Guise. How it Began: The One Push-up Challenge
2. I've written 35,000 word stories that I would call "short novels" if I had to call them anything, but 40-50k is generally accepted as the boundary between novellas and novels.
3. http://creativethinking.net/

## 6. Julio

1. https://www.webmd.com/diet/caffeine-myths-and-facts#1

## 7. Your Reward

1. Tip: before you settle on a title, check that Amazon doesn't assume it's a mistype when you search for it. My first book was called *Stryke First* (Stryke being the name of the hero), but Amazon assumed that the searcher meant "Strike", and so my book wouldn't appear since its title wasn't *Strike First*. Until I changed it. Twice.

## 9. Making it Easy

1. These are plots of land owned by the local government and split up into tiny parcels that are rented out to locals to grow vegetables.

## 10. Your Writing Environment

1. I'm only kidding – many people say they find it easier to be creative with the tactile feedback of handwriting. For me, it would be an exercise in frustration both because I'd then have to type it in, but also because I can't read my own writing...
2. Are you old enough/geeky enough/British enough to remember the Amstrad PCW? What a wonderful device. I'm slightly tempted to buy an old one, but I suspect, like when you meet your heroes, I'd be disappointed
3. Although in the case of this book, the first draft was written using the browser-based version of Word because it supports footnotes and most of the alternatives don't.

## Introduction

1. One of those most of us agree on is: always use an editor

## 20. What should I write?

1. https://www.kevpartner.co.uk/klytics/ - the monthly membership is expensive, but the individual genre reports are great value

## 22. How long should my book be?

1. You're not JRR Tolkien either
2. Six, in fact: three volumes, each containing two books

## 23. Basic Story Structure

1. *Harry Potter and the Sorcerer's Stone* in the US, for some reason

## 24. Which software should I use for my first draft?

1. https://www.kevpartner.co.uk/novlr-novel-writing-software/
2. https://www.dabblewriter.com/
3. Google Docs also supports footnotes, by the way

## 25. Keeping Notes

1. keep.google.com

## 26. Do you need an editor?

1. Note that I don't use the serial/Oxford comma. My approach is to use it only when essential for clarity. And because leaving it out is my way of torturing my editors.
2. Always remember, it's **your** book, not your editor's

## 27. Types of editor

1. https://www.chicagomanualofstyle.org/home.html
2. Hint – if you think you need a comma, you probably don't

3. A dev editor or line editor **must** be experienced in your genre. A copy editor can be more of a generalist
4. Search "SPF Community" on Facebook to find an excellent group to join

Printed in Great Britain
by Amazon